AF840811

The Smart Borrower's Home Equity Blueprint

How to Unlock Your Home's True Financial Power with a Licensed Broker

By Joseph G. Correa

Licensed Mortgage Broker, Finibi Mortgage

Copyright & Legal Notice

First Edition, 2026

Table of Contents

Foreword

For most homeowners, home equity is invisible. They see a number on a statement, or a rough estimate on a website, but they do not understand how that equity behaves inside the financial system. Banks see your equity as an asset that can be leveraged, securitized, and risk-managed. Investors see it as a form of low-cost capital. Yet most homeowners treat it emotionally instead of strategically, only thinking about it when money is tight or when an emergency appears. The smart borrower thinks about equity the way a business owner thinks about a line of credit: something that must be structured, timed, and optimized. This book will show you how to shift your mindset from homeowner to equity manager, so you can decide when to borrow, when to hold, when to deploy, and when to protect what you have built.

One of the most dangerous myths in personal finance is that having access to money means you should use it. A HELOC is not wealth. Equity is not profit. Access to capital is only valuable when it is paired with intelligence. Over the course of this series, you have seen how powerful home equity can be when used for real estate, business, debt restructuring, and cash flow creation. You have also learned how quickly that same power can become dangerous when interest rates rise, income changes, or property values fluctuate. The smart borrower understands both sides of this equation. This blueprint is not about borrowing more. It is about borrowing better. It is about creating a structure where every dollar of equity you access is aligned with a purpose, a timeline, and a risk boundary that protects your home and your future.

This is also the book where the role of a licensed mortgage broker becomes central. Most people believe their bank is their financial partner, but in reality, banks only offer their own products. They do not compare the market. They do not design multi-lender strategies. They do not build equity roadmaps. A broker does. A professional broker does not just quote a rate — they analyze how your equity fits into your full financial picture, including income type, tax strategy, business ownership, real estate goals, credit profile, and risk tolerance. The smart borrower does not shop for loans the way people shop for credit cards. They build long-term relationships with professionals who understand how to structure access to capital in a way that evolves as their life changes. This book shows you how to think like that professional so you can never be taken advantage of by incomplete advice or one-size-fits-all lending.

Throughout this series, you have been introduced to dozens of ways equity can be used: velocity banking, BRRR investing, business funding, passive income, emergency reserves, renovation capital, and tax-efficient borrowing. What separates amateurs from professionals is not which tool they use — it is whether those tools are coordinated. The Smart Borrower's Home Equity Blueprint is about orchestration. It is about building a system where your HELOC, your mortgage, your credit profile, your property values, and your income streams are all working together. When structured correctly, your home becomes not just a place to live, but a financial engine that adapts to economic cycles, interest rate changes, and life events.

You will also learn that the most powerful form of home equity is the equity you never have to touch. A properly structured equity position improves your negotiating power, your borrowing cost, and your financial flexibility even when the balance is zero. Just like a business credit line improves a company's stability, a strategically maintained HELOC improves a household's financial resilience. Smart borrowers do not wait until they need money to apply. They build access when times are good, so they are protected when times are not. This book teaches you how to maintain that readiness without falling into the trap of unnecessary debt.

As you reach the end of this series, it is important to understand that this knowledge is not theoretical. Everything you have read is built on real lending guidelines, real underwriting rules, real credit behavior, and real market conditions. Home equity is one of the few financial tools available to everyday people that allows them to borrow at institutional-level interest rates while maintaining control of their assets. That opportunity comes with responsibility. The goal of this final book is to make sure you carry forward not just tactics, but wisdom — the ability to know when to act and when not to.

This blueprint is not about maximizing leverage. It is about maximizing freedom. When your equity is structured correctly, you are less dependent on banks, less vulnerable to income shocks, and more capable of seizing opportunities when they appear. You can move faster, invest smarter, and sleep better at night because your home is no longer a passive asset. It is part of a deliberate financial design. That is what it means to be a smart borrower, and that is what this final book exists to give you.

By the time you finish *The Smart Borrower's Home Equity Blueprint*, you will not simply understand HELOCs, lenders, or home equity products. You will understand how to think like the financial system that uses them. And when you understand how the system works, you stop being controlled by it — you begin using it.

Chapter 1

Designing Your Personal Home Equity Blueprint

A smart borrower does not begin with a loan application. They begin with a blueprint. Before any numbers are run, before any documents are uploaded, and before any lender is contacted, the borrower who builds long-term wealth with home equity starts by understanding their financial structure. A home is not just a place to live; it is a balance sheet. On one side is the value of the property. On the other side is the debt attached to it. The difference between those two numbers is equity, and equity is a form of stored financial energy. When you borrow against it, you are releasing that energy into the world. If you release it without a plan, it disappears into consumption, interest, and financial stress. If you release it with a blueprint, it turns into leverage, cash flow, and long-term wealth.

The blueprint begins by identifying three core categories of equity usage: defensive, productive, and opportunistic. Defensive equity protects your life and finances. This includes emergency reserves, medical buffers, job transition cushions, and tax reserves. Productive equity is used to create income or reduce expensive debt, such as paying off high-interest credit cards, funding a business, or investing in real estate.

Opportunistic equity is used when the right deal or market window appears, such as buying a discounted property, acquiring a business, or funding a time-sensitive investment. Smart borrowers allocate their equity across all three categories instead of dumping it into one. This creates stability, growth, and flexibility at the same time.

Most homeowners make the mistake of thinking in terms of how much they can borrow. Smart borrowers think in terms of how much they should deploy. Your equity limit is not your spending limit. It is your strategic capacity. The blueprint teaches you to first decide how much equity stays untouched as a safety buffer. That buffer protects you if values drop, income changes, or rates rise. A conservative smart borrower may choose to never use more than 60 to 70 percent of their available equity even if the lender approves them for more. This is how wealth is preserved through economic cycles.

Another foundational concept is the separation of capital and consumption. Borrowed equity should rarely be used for depreciating items like vacations, cars, or lifestyle upgrades. Those purchases produce no return and permanently convert your equity into expense. The blueprint instead assigns borrowed equity to assets or financial moves that either produce cash flow, reduce high-interest debt, or increase net worth. This is how homeowners become investors without needing outside capital.

A key part of your blueprint is understanding your income structure. W-2 income, self-employed income, rental income, and business income are all treated differently by lenders, and that affects how your equity can be accessed. Smart borrowers structure their income and tax returns in a way that supports future borrowing, even if it means paying slightly more in taxes today to gain access to hundreds of thousands of dollars in low-cost capital tomorrow. The blueprint connects income strategy to equity access.

Timing is another invisible force that determines success or failure. Equity should be established before it is needed. The best HELOCs are opened when income is strong, credit is high, and markets are stable. Once open, they can be kept unused for years until the right opportunity appears. Borrowers who wait until they are in financial stress almost always get worse terms or get denied completely. The blueprint therefore includes not just how much to borrow, but when to secure access.

Interest rate management is also built into the design. Smart borrowers understand that HELOC rates fluctuate and that rising rates increase risk. They use fixed-rate options, partial paydowns, and cash flow planning to control how interest impacts their finances. A HELOC is not meant to be permanently maxed out. It is meant to be recycled, paid down, and reused as capital rotates through investments and debt strategies.

Your blueprint also accounts for property value growth. As homes appreciate, equity increases. Smart borrowers periodically review their property values and adjust their credit lines accordingly. This allows their financial capacity to grow alongside the market without needing to refinance. This is one of the most powerful wealth multipliers available to homeowners.

Finally, the blueprint includes an exit plan. Every use of equity must include a repayment or payoff strategy. Whether it is rental income, business profits, property sales, or future refinancing, every dollar borrowed must have a path back home. This prevents equity from turning into permanent debt and ensures the homeowner stays in control.

By the end of this chapter, you should no longer see your house as a static asset. You should see it as a living financial system, one that must be designed, monitored, and optimized just like any successful business.

Practical Example: *Building a Real Home Equity Blueprint with Numbers*

Imagine a homeowner named Alex who owns a property worth $600,000. Alex owes $350,000 on the first mortgage. To calculate equity, we subtract the loan balance from the value. $600,000 minus $350,000 equals $250,000 in total equity. Most banks will allow borrowing up to 80 percent of the home's value. Eighty percent of $600,000 is $480,000. If Alex already owes $350,000, then $480,000 minus $350,000 equals $130,000 of available HELOC credit.

Alex is approved for a $130,000 HELOC, but as a smart borrower, Alex does not plan to use all of it. Alex decides to keep 30 percent of that line as a permanent safety buffer. Thirty percent of $130,000 is $39,000. That means Alex will only use $91,000 for actual strategies. This protects Alex if home values drop or income changes.

Alex now divides the $91,000 into three buckets. Forty percent goes to defensive capital, forty percent to productive capital, and twenty percent to opportunistic capital. Forty percent of $91,000 is $36,400. That goes into a savings account as an emergency fund. Another $36,400 goes toward productive uses, and the remaining $18,200 is reserved for opportunities. Alex has $28,000 in credit card debt at 22 percent interest. By using $28,000 from the productive bucket, Alex wipes out the credit cards. The interest on the HELOC is 8 percent. On $28,000, 8 percent is $2,240 per year. On credit cards at 22 percent, $28,000 would have cost $6,160 per year. By shifting the debt, Alex saves $3,920 per year in interest alone.

That leaves $8,400 in the productive bucket. Alex uses this as a down payment on a small rental property that produces $500 per month in cash flow. That is $6,000 per year. Even after accounting for $800 per year in HELOC interest on the $8,400, Alex nets $5,200 annually.

Now Alex looks at the opportunistic bucket of $18,200. Alex leaves this untouched, waiting for a discounted property, business acquisition, or emergency investment. Meanwhile, the defensive $36,400 sits in savings, creating stability.

Let's add everything up. Alex eliminated $28,000 in high-interest debt, saving $3,920 per year. Alex created $6,000 per year in rental income. The HELOC interest on the $36,400 used is $2,912 per year at 8 percent. When we subtract the interest from the income and savings, Alex is still ahead by $6, + $3,920 minus $2,912, which equals $6, + $1,008? Let's calculate properly. Rental income of $6,000 plus interest savings of $3,920 equals $9,920. Subtract HELOC interest of $2,912 and Alex nets $7,008 per year. Alex now has $36,400 in cash reserves, $18,200 in available opportunity capital, $28,000 of credit card debt gone, and a rental producing income. This is how a blueprint turns equity into a self-reinforcing financial system instead of a risky loan.

This is what it means to be a smart borrower.

Chapter 2

Structuring the Perfect HELOC for Maximum Control

A HELOC is not a single product; it is a structure. The difference between a borrower who struggles with rising payments and one who thrives with flexibility is not how much they borrowed, but how their line of credit was designed. In this chapter, the goal is to teach you how to build a HELOC that behaves like a professional financing tool instead of a consumer loan. The smart borrower thinks in terms of credit architecture, not just credit limits. That architecture includes the size of the line, how interest is calculated, whether balances can be fixed, how payments are applied, and how the line can be segmented for different purposes.

The first pillar of HELOC structure is separation. A single undifferentiated credit line creates chaos because money from different uses becomes mixed together. Smart borrowers either open multiple HELOCs or create sub-accounts and tracking categories inside one HELOC so that every dollar has a job. Debt payoff balances are tracked separately from investment balances. Emergency funds are tracked separately from opportunity capital. This allows the borrower to see exactly what is happening with their money at all times and prevents the psychological trap of treating borrowed money as free cash.

The second pillar is payment control. Most people accept the minimum payment on a HELOC, which is usually interest-only during the draw period. Smart borrowers go further. They design a payment plan that forces their balances down over time. This could mean paying principal monthly, sending rental income directly into the HELOC, or using business profits to reduce balances. The result is that the line becomes more powerful over time instead of more dangerous. Every dollar paid down becomes new available credit that can be redeployed.

The third pillar is interest rate management. HELOCs have variable rates, which means risk increases when rates rise. Smart borrowers limit that risk by using fixed-rate conversion options, maintaining unused credit as a buffer, and avoiding long-term dependence on floating balances. If you plan to hold a balance for years, converting it to a fixed-rate segment stabilizes your payment and protects you from market volatility. If you plan to use funds short-term, keeping them variable allows you to pay them off quickly without penalties.

The fourth pillar is cash flow integration. A HELOC should be integrated into how money flows through your life. Paychecks, rental income, business revenue, and even tax refunds can be routed through the HELOC so that idle cash reduces interest while it waits to be used. This makes every dollar work harder. The HELOC becomes a financial hub instead of a debt.

The fifth pillar is growth alignment. As your home appreciates and your income grows, your HELOC should grow with you. Smart borrowers review their property value every one to two years and request limit increases when appropriate. This allows their financial capacity to expand without refinancing or restarting their mortgage. It also preserves their interest rate and amortization on the primary loan.

Finally, structure includes discipline. A HELOC is powerful because it is flexible. That same flexibility can destroy people who lack rules. The smart borrower sets borrowing limits, purpose rules, and review schedules. They never allow their HELOC balance to drift upward without intention. This is how a HELOC becomes a long-term wealth engine instead of a financial trap.

Practical Example: *Structuring a HELOC for Maximum Control*

Let's look at how this works with real numbers. Sarah owns a home worth $750,000 and owes $400,000 on her first mortgage. Eighty percent of $750,000 is $600,000.

Subtracting the mortgage balance of $400,000 leaves $200,000 available for a HELOC. Sarah opens a $200,000 line but decides to only use 60 percent of it. Sixty percent of $200,000 is $120,000. That leaves $80,000 unused as a permanent safety buffer.

Sarah divides the $120,000 into three segments. $50,000 is for debt restructuring, $40,000 is for investments, and $30,000 is for emergency and opportunity reserves. Sarah has $45,000 in credit cards at 21 percent interest. She uses $45,000 from the debt segment to pay them off. At 21 percent, $45,000 would cost $9,450 per year in interest. Her HELOC rate is 8 percent, which costs $3,600 per year on the same balance. That saves Sarah $5,850 annually.

Sarah uses $30,000 from the investment segment as a down payment on a rental that generates $800 per month in net cash flow. That is $9,600 per year. The HELOC interest on $30,000 at 8 percent is $2,400. After interest, Sarah still makes $7,200 annually from that investment.

Sarah leaves the remaining $10,000 of her investment bucket and the full $30,000 reserve bucket untouched. That $40,000 is liquid, available, and not accruing interest.

Let's add up Sarah's results. She saved $5,850 per year by refinancing her credit cards. She earns $9,600 from the rental.

That totals $15,450. She pays $3,600 in interest on the $45,000 balance and $2,400 on the $30,000 balance, totaling $6,000. $15,450 minus $6,000 equals $9,450 in net annual gain.

Sarah now has zero credit card debt, a rental producing income, $40,000 in reserves, and $80,000 in unused HELOC credit protecting her home. That is what proper structure looks like in real life.

Chapter 3

Using Home Equity to Build Compounding Wealth

The difference between people who stay financially stuck and those who quietly become wealthy almost always comes down to whether their money compounds. Compounding means that one dollar produces another dollar, which then produces another, and over time the growth accelerates. Home equity is one of the few financial tools that allows ordinary homeowners to access large amounts of low-cost capital that can be deployed into compounding assets. This chapter teaches you how to use that capital correctly so that your equity does not simply move from one account to another, but instead creates a multiplying effect across your financial life.

Most people think of borrowing as something that makes them poorer because it adds debt. Smart borrowers understand that debt used for consumption is dangerous, but debt used for productive assets can increase net worth. When home equity is invested into assets that generate income or appreciate in value, that equity does not disappear — it transforms. A rental property, a business, or a cash-flowing investment becomes a new asset that continues producing long after the original borrowed dollars are paid back. This is how homeowners build wealth faster than people who rely only on savings.

The key principle is that every borrowed dollar must either generate income, reduce higher-interest debt, or increase asset value. If it does not do at least one of those things, it is not compounding — it is eroding. Smart borrowers look at every potential use of their HELOC through this lens. They ask whether the borrowed money will create a return greater than the interest cost. If the answer is yes and the risk is controlled, it belongs in the compounding portfolio.

Real estate is the most common compounding engine for home equity because it offers leverage, cash flow, tax benefits, and appreciation at the same time. When you use a HELOC as a down payment or renovation fund, you are controlling a much larger asset than the amount you borrowed. That asset produces rent, increases in value, and eventually can be refinanced or sold to repay the HELOC while leaving you with equity and income. This is why experienced investors call home equity the "seed capital" for property portfolios.

Businesses can also be powerful compounding tools when chosen correctly. A service business, an online business, or a franchise funded with equity can generate profits far beyond the interest cost. The smart borrower, however, never uses equity for speculative ventures without cash flow or a clear path to repayment. The blueprint always requires that borrowed funds produce reliable income that can service the debt and build wealth at the same time.

Compounding also happens through interest savings. Paying off 20-plus percent credit card debt with an 8-percent HELOC instantly creates a guaranteed return equal to the difference. That freed-up cash flow can then be invested or used to pay down principal faster, which further accelerates growth. The smart borrower sees debt optimization as part of their compounding strategy, not just a way to feel relief.

Another layer of compounding comes from recycling. When income from investments is sent back into the HELOC, balances drop and available credit increases. That new available credit can be redeployed into more income-producing assets. This cycle allows one HELOC to fund multiple investments over time without needing to refinance or inject new cash.

The most important part of compounding with home equity is patience and discipline. This is not a get-rich-quick strategy. It is a system for turning a static asset into a dynamic wealth engine. When used carefully, your home does not just store value — it creates it.

Practical Example: *Turning One HELOC into a Compounding Wealth Engine*

Let's look at how compounding works in real life. Mark owns a home worth $500,000 and owes $300,000 on his mortgage. Eighty percent of $500,000 is $400,000. Subtracting the mortgage leaves $100,000 available for a HELOC. Mark opens a $100,000 HELOC and decides to only use $70,000 so he has a $30,000 safety buffer.

Mark uses $50,000 of the HELOC as a down payment and renovation fund on a small duplex that costs $250,000. The duplex rents for $2,400 per month. After mortgage, taxes, insurance, and maintenance, Mark nets $900 per month. That equals $10,800 per year. The HELOC interest on $50,000 at 8 percent is $4,000 per year. That leaves Mark with $6,800 in net cash flow.

Mark uses another $15,000 from the HELOC to pay off credit cards that were charging 22 percent interest. On $15,000, that would have been $3,300 per year. On the HELOC at 8 percent, it costs $1,200. Mark saves $2,100 per year in interest.

Now let's add everything up. Mark earns $10,800 from the duplex. He saves $2,100 from interest reduction. That equals $12,900 in financial gain. He pays $4,000 in HELOC interest on the duplex funds and $1,200 on the credit card balance, totaling $5,200. Subtracting $5,200 from $12,900 leaves Mark with $7,700 in net annual benefit.

Mark sends that $7,700 into the HELOC every year. After the first year, his $65,000 HELOC balance drops to $57,300. That creates more available credit. Over time, as rents rise and Mark continues paying down the HELOC, his available equity grows while his income increases.

This is compounding. The same equity is working in multiple places at once — producing rent, saving interest, and regenerating credit — all while Mark's home and rental property continue appreciating. This is how smart borrowers turn equity into wealth.

Chapter 4

Managing Risk, Cash Flow and Market Cycles

Wealth built with leverage is powerful, but leverage without risk management is dangerous. This chapter exists because every financial crisis, every foreclosure wave, and every investor collapse has had one thing in common: people used debt without understanding cycles. Smart borrowers do not fear leverage, but they respect it. Home equity gives you access to capital, but capital must be controlled, buffered, and protected against changes in interest rates, income, and property values. This chapter teaches you how to keep your home equity system safe no matter what the economy does.

The first rule of risk management is liquidity. Liquidity means the ability to survive without selling assets or missing payments. A HELOC without a cash buffer is a ticking clock. Smart borrowers keep part of their line unused and part of their borrowed funds sitting in cash. This ensures that even if income stops, investments slow, or tenants move out, the homeowner can still make every payment on time. Cash is not idle when it protects leverage. It is insurance. The second rule is interest-rate awareness. HELOCs are variable-rate products. When rates rise, payments rise. Smart borrowers assume that rates will go up, not stay flat. That means they never use so much equity that a rate increase would force financial distress. They also convert long-term balances to fixed-rate segments when available, locking in predictable payments and removing uncertainty from their plan.

The third rule is debt coverage. Every investment funded with equity must generate enough income to cover its share of the HELOC payment. This ensures that even if personal income drops, the asset itself pays for the money used to create it. This is how professionals avoid being personally trapped by their own leverage.

The fourth rule is value protection. Home prices move in cycles. Smart borrowers never assume today's value will last forever. They borrow conservatively so that even if values drop 15 to 25 percent, they are not underwater. This is why they keep unused credit and do not push loan-to-value limits.

The fifth rule is diversification. A smart borrower never ties all equity to one property, one business, or one strategy. They spread risk across multiple income streams so no single failure can destroy their financial system. Finally, smart borrowers stress-test their numbers. They ask what happens if rent drops, if interest rises, if expenses increase, or if income pauses. If the plan still works under stress, it is safe. If it breaks, it is redesigned.

Practical Example: *Stress-Testing a Home Equity Strategy*

David owns a home worth $700,000 with a $420,000 mortgage. Eighty percent of $700,000 is $560,000. Subtracting the mortgage gives him $140,000 available for a HELOC. David opens the line but decides to only use $90,000, keeping $50,000 unused as safety.

David uses $60,000 to invest in a rental property that produces $1,200 per month in net cash flow. That is $14,400 per year. The HELOC interest on $60,000 at 8 percent is $4,800. That leaves $9,600 in net income.

David uses another $20,000 to pay off credit cards at 24 percent. On $20,000, that would be $4,800 per year. On the HELOC at 8 percent, it costs $1,600. That saves him $3,200 per year.

David leaves $10,000 of his used HELOC in cash. This acts as an emergency buffer.

Now let's add everything. David earns $14,400 in rental income and saves $3,200 in interest. That totals $17,600. He pays $4,800 in interest on the rental funds and $1,600 on the credit card funds, totaling $6,400. $17,600 minus $6,400 equals $11,200 in net annual benefit.

Now stress test it. If rates rise to 10 percent, interest on $80,000 becomes $8,000 instead of $6,400. That reduces net income to $9,600. David is still positive. If rent drops by 20 percent, rental income falls from $14,400 to $11,520. Even then, after interest, David is still cash-flow positive.

Because David kept $50,000 unused and $10,000 in cash, he is protected. This is how smart borrowers survive market cycles while others fail.

Chapter 5

Turning Home Equity Into a Permanent Financial Engine

The most powerful difference between people who merely use home equity and people who build wealth with it is whether their system lasts. One-time borrowing does not create financial freedom. A permanent financial engine does. This chapter is about designing a structure where your home equity does not get spent and disappear, but instead becomes a self-replenishing source of capital that grows stronger every year. This is the stage where homeowners stop thinking in terms of transactions and begin thinking in terms of financial machinery.

A permanent equity engine is built on three forces working together: cash flow, principal reduction, and credit regeneration. Cash flow comes from investments and debt savings. Principal reduction happens when those cash flows are used to pay down balances. Credit regeneration happens when paid-down balances reopen available HELOC capacity. When these three forces are aligned, one dollar of equity can be used over and over again without being permanently consumed. This is what separates amateurs from professionals. Most people use a HELOC the same way they use a credit card. They borrow, they make minimum payments, and the balance lingers for years. That approach turns equity into a liability. The smart borrower designs a system where borrowed funds are always attached to something that pays them back. Rental income, business profits, interest savings, or tax refunds all flow back into the HELOC. This causes balances to shrink and capacity to grow.

The next layer is velocity. Velocity means how fast money moves through your system. The faster cash enters and exits the HELOC, the less interest you pay and the more powerful the line becomes. Smart borrowers route income through their HELOC because every dollar that touches it reduces interest for that day. Over time, this creates thousands of dollars in savings that can be redeployed into investments or debt reduction.

Another key element is reinvestment. When an investment funded by equity produces profit, that profit should not be spent. It should be used to pay down the HELOC or fund the next asset. This creates a chain reaction where each deal funds the next. This is how one property turns into two, then four, then eight, without injecting new cash.

A permanent engine also requires maintenance. Smart borrowers regularly review their balances, interest rates, property values, and cash flows. They adjust strategies when markets shift. They refinance investments when needed. They increase HELOC limits as their homes appreciate. This keeps the engine tuned and growing.

Finally, the system must always protect the home. The house is the foundation of the engine. Smart borrowers never allow equity usage to endanger their primary residence. They keep buffers, maintain cash reserves, and ensure all borrowed funds have income attached. This keeps the engine alive through recessions, job changes, and market cycles.

Practical Example: *Building a Permanent Equity Engine*

Let's see how this works in real life. Maria owns a home worth $800,000 and owes $500,000 on her mortgage. Eighty percent of $800,000 is $640,000. Subtracting the mortgage leaves $140,000 available for a HELOC. Maria opens a $140,000 line but only plans to use $90,000, leaving $50,000 unused as protection.

Maria uses $60,000 to purchase and renovate a small rental that produces $1,500 per month in net cash flow. That equals $18,000 per year. The HELOC interest on $60,000 at 8 percent is $4,800. That leaves $13,200 in net cash flow.

Maria uses another $20,000 to eliminate high-interest credit card debt. Those cards were costing 20 percent interest, or $4,000 per year. On the HELOC at 8 percent, that balance costs $1,600. That saves her $2,400 per year.

Maria leaves $10,000 of her used HELOC in cash as an emergency reserve.

Now let's add everything together. Maria earns $18,000 from her rental and saves $2,400 from interest reduction, for a total benefit of $20,400. She pays $4,800 in interest on the rental funds and $1,600 on the credit card funds, totaling $6,400. $20,400 minus $6,400 equals $14,000 in net annual cash flow.

Maria sends that $14,000 into the HELOC. After the first year, her $80,000 HELOC balance drops to $66,000. That creates $14,000 in new available credit. That new credit can now be used to fund another investment, while the first rental continues producing cash.

Over time, Maria's equity regenerates, her income grows, and her HELOC becomes a permanent financial engine instead of a one-time loan. This is how smart borrowers build wealth that lasts.

Chapter 6

Scaling Your Equity System Without Increasing Risk

At some point, a smart borrower moves beyond using home equity for one deal or one improvement and begins to think in terms of scale. Scaling does not mean borrowing more recklessly. It means increasing the output of your system without increasing the danger to your home. This chapter teaches how to expand your income, investments, and borrowing power while keeping risk contained. The goal is not to use more leverage, but to use leverage more intelligently.

The first principle of safe scaling is income-first growth. Your system should never grow faster than the cash flow supporting it. If a rental produces $1,000 per month, only part of that should be used to expand. The rest must be reserved for maintenance, vacancies, and interest increases. Smart borrowers never allow new investments to depend on best-case assumptions. They expand only when existing assets are already overperforming their obligations.

The second principle is credit recycling. When a HELOC is used to fund an asset, that asset's income should be used to pay down the HELOC. As the balance drops, the available credit rises. That newly available credit can then be used for the next opportunity. This allows one HELOC to fund multiple investments over time without permanently increasing debt. This is how portfolios grow without adding strain.

The third principle is asset stacking. Instead of placing all equity into one large deal, smart borrowers use multiple smaller assets that each produce income. This spreads risk. If one tenant leaves or one business slows, the rest continue paying. This makes the system resilient.

The fourth principle is interest containment. As balances grow, interest becomes more powerful. Smart borrowers lock portions of their HELOC into fixed rates when balances will be held long-term. They also use cash flow to keep balances falling even while scaling.

The fifth principle is equity preservation. Even as income and assets grow, the homeowner must always keep a cushion of unused credit and home equity. This protects against downturns, appraisals, and emergencies. A scaled system without buffers is fragile.

The final principle is periodic optimization. Properties get refinanced, rents rise, credit improves, and HELOC limits can be increased. Smart borrowers periodically restructure their system so that old assets free up new capital. This keeps growth moving without stress.

Practical Example: *Scaling Without Taking on More Risk*

Let's look at a real example. James owns a home worth $900,000 and owes $540,000 on his mortgage. Eighty percent of $900,000 is $720,000. Subtracting the mortgage leaves $180,000 available for a HELOC. James opens a $180,000 HELOC but only uses $110,000, leaving $70,000 unused as safety.

James uses $60,000 to buy a rental that produces $1,400 per month in net cash flow. That is $16,800 per year. The HELOC interest on $60,000 at 8 percent is $4,800, leaving $12,000 net.

James uses another $30,000 to buy a second rental that produces $900 per month in net cash flow, or $10,800 per year. The interest on $30,000 at 8 percent is $2,400, leaving $8,400 net.

James uses $20,000 to eliminate credit card debt that was charging 21 percent interest. On $20,000, that would be $4,200 per year. On the HELOC at 8 percent, it costs $1,600. That saves $2,600 per year.

Now let's add everything up. James earns $16,800 plus $10,800, which equals $27,600 in rental income. He saves

$2,600 in interest. That equals $30,200 in benefit. He pays $4,800 plus $2,400 plus $1,600 in HELOC interest, totaling $8,800. $30,200 minus $8,800 equals $21,400 in net annual gain.

James sends that $21,400 into the HELOC. After the first year, his $110,000 balance drops to $88,600. That creates $21,400 in new available credit. His rentals still exist, his income still flows, and his risk is lower than when he started.

That is what safe scaling looks like.

Chapter 7

Exit Strategies, Payoff Planning, and Lifetime Control

The ultimate purpose of using home equity is not to stay in debt forever, but to gain control over your financial life. A smart borrower always knows how every borrowed dollar will eventually return home. This chapter focuses on exit strategies, payoff planning, and how to structure your system so that leverage serves you for decades without ever putting your home at risk. Without exit planning, even profitable strategies eventually collapse. With it, even modest investments can create generational wealth.

The first rule of exit strategy is clarity. Every HELOC balance must have a defined source of repayment. That source can be rental income, business profit, asset sales, or refinancing. What matters is that it is planned. Smart borrowers never let balances float indefinitely without knowing where the money to pay them off will come from. This prevents emotional decisions when markets shift.

The second rule is layering. You should never rely on only one exit path. A rental funded with equity should have at least three possible exits: cash flow payoff over time, refinance after appreciation, or sale of the property. A business funded with equity should be able to pay back the loan through profits, resale of the business, or refinancing of the home. Layered exits create safety.

The third rule is amortization control. Smart borrowers do not accept interest-only payments forever. They design principal reduction into their system. Even small monthly reductions dramatically reduce risk over time and accelerate wealth. The goal is not just to earn income, but to turn borrowed money back into equity.

The fourth rule is cycle awareness. Economic cycles affect interest rates, property values, and buyer demand. Smart borrowers exit or refinance when conditions are favorable, not when they are desperate. This requires planning years in advance.

The fifth rule is asset harvesting. Over time, some investments will grow more than others. Smart borrowers periodically sell or refinance winning assets to replenish equity and fund new opportunities. This keeps their portfolio fresh and efficient.

The final rule is home protection. The primary residence must always remain safe. No strategy is worth risking the roof over your head. Smart borrowers maintain equity buffers, insurance, and cash reserves so that no single event can force a sale.

Practical Example: *Designing Exit Strategies with Real Numbers*

Let's look at how exit planning works. Linda owns a home worth $850,000 and owes $520,000. Eighty percent of $850,000 is $680,000. Subtracting the mortgage leaves $160,000 available for a HELOC. Linda opens a $160,000 HELOC but uses only $100,000, keeping $60,000 unused as protection.

Linda uses $70,000 to buy and renovate a rental property. It produces $1,600 per month in net cash flow, which is $19,200 per year. The HELOC interest on $70,000 at 8 percent is $5,600. That leaves $13,600 in net income.

Linda uses another $20,000 to eliminate credit card debt at 23 percent. On $20,000, that would have cost $4,600 per year. On the HELOC at 8 percent, it costs $1,600. That saves $3,000 per year.

Linda keeps $10,000 in cash.

Now let's add everything. Linda earns $19,200 from rent and saves $3,000 in interest, for a total benefit of $22,200. She pays $5,600 plus $1,600 in HELOC interest, totaling $7,200. $22,200 minus $7,200 equals $15,000 in net annual gain.

Linda uses that $15,000 each year to pay down the HELOC. In about 7 years, the $90,000 balance is gone. At that point, Linda still owns the rental, which may now be worth more, and her HELOC is fully restored. She can then either keep the rental for cash flow or sell it and reclaim even more equity. This is how smart borrowers exit while growing richer.

Chapter 8

Turning Equity Into Lifestyle Freedom Without Breaking the System

Wealth is not just about accumulating assets; it is about buying freedom. The reason people pursue financial independence is not to see a bigger number on a screen, but to gain control over their time, their choices, and their stress. Home equity, when used intelligently, can give you that freedom long before you reach traditional retirement age. The mistake most people make is trying to use equity to escape work instead of using it to build systems that replace work. This chapter teaches you how to turn equity into lifestyle freedom without damaging the engine that produces it.

The first principle is separating income from labor. True freedom comes when money flows whether you show up or not. Equity should be deployed into assets that continue paying you even when you take time off. Rentals, dividend-producing investments, small businesses with management in place, and digital income streams are ideal because they detach your time from your income. Smart borrowers use equity to buy systems, not jobs. The second principle is protecting your core. Your home and your HELOC are the foundation of your system. Lifestyle spending should never be funded directly from borrowed equity. Instead, lifestyle upgrades should come from the income produced by equity-funded assets. This ensures that your freedom is sustainable instead of temporary.

The third principle is smoothing cash flow. One of the most powerful uses of a HELOC is creating stability during transitions. Whether you are starting a business, taking time off, or changing careers, a properly structured equity system can provide predictable cash flow that reduces stress and allows better decision-making.

The fourth principle is tax efficiency. Interest on borrowed funds used for investment or business purposes is often tax-deductible. This means the real cost of borrowing can be much lower than the stated rate. Smart borrowers coordinate their equity strategy with their tax strategy so more of their income stays in their pocket.

The fifth principle is lifestyle scaling. As income grows, lifestyle can grow — but only in proportion to passive income, not borrowed funds. This keeps freedom permanent.

The final principle is optionality. When your equity engine is working, you are no longer forced to accept bad deals, bad jobs, or bad timing. You can wait for the right opportunity because your system is supporting you.

Practical Example: *Using Equity to Buy Time and Freedom*

Let's look at how lifestyle freedom works with real numbers. Kevin owns a home worth $780,000 and owes $480,000. Eighty percent of $780,000 is $624,000. Subtracting the mortgage leaves $144,000 available for a HELOC. Kevin opens a $144,000 HELOC but uses only $90,000, leaving $54,000 unused for safety.

Kevin uses $70,000 to purchase two small rental properties that together generate $2,200 per month in net cash flow. That equals $26,400 per year. The HELOC interest on $70,000 at 8 percent is $5,600, leaving $20,800 net.

Kevin uses another $10,000 to invest in a small online business that produces $500 per month in profit, or $6,000 per year. The interest on $10,000 at 8 percent is $800, leaving $5,200 net.

Kevin keeps $10,000 in cash.

Now let's add everything. Kevin earns $26,400 from rentals and $6,000 from the online business, for a total of $32,400. He pays $5,600 plus $800 in interest, totaling $6,400. $32,400 minus $6,400 equals $26,000 in net annual income.

Kevin uses $20,000 of that to replace part of his job income, allowing him to reduce his work hours. He uses the remaining $6,000 to pay down the HELOC. Over time, the HELOC balance drops, available credit rises, and Kevin's passive income grows. This is how equity buys freedom without destroying the system.

Chapter 9

Long-Term Protection, Legacy, and Passing Wealth Forward

The ultimate purpose of using home equity wisely is not just to create income for yourself, but to create security, opportunity, and freedom for the people who come after you. When home equity is structured correctly, it becomes one of the most powerful legacy tools available to ordinary families. This chapter is about shifting your thinking from short-term wealth to multigenerational stability. Smart borrowers do not just ask how much money they can make, they ask how long that money will last and who it will serve.

Most families lose wealth within one or two generations because assets are not structured to survive inheritance, taxes, and life changes. Home equity, when paired with income-producing assets, creates a self-renewing pool of capital that can outlive the original owner. Rentals, businesses, and investment accounts funded by equity can continue paying long after the original loan is gone. This is how a house becomes more than a home — it becomes a financial anchor for an entire family.

The first pillar of legacy planning is ownership. Assets funded with equity must be held in a way that allows them to be transferred, protected, and managed by heirs. This often means using trusts, LLCs, or beneficiary designations so that income streams continue without interruption. Smart borrowers coordinate their equity strategy with estate planning so nothing is left to chance.

The second pillar is debt control. A powerful legacy is one where assets remain but debt disappears. The goal is to use income from equity-funded assets to pay off the HELOC and mortgage over time so that future generations inherit property and income without the burden of loans. This creates true generational wealth.

The third pillar is education. Your children or heirs must understand how the system works. A HELOC strategy that is not understood can be dismantled in a single generation. Smart borrowers leave behind not just assets, but instructions.

The fourth pillar is income continuity. Rentals, businesses, and investment accounts must be managed so that income continues through ownership changes. This may involve professional management or family governance structures.

The fifth pillar is protection. Insurance, reserves, and diversification keep legacy assets safe from lawsuits, disasters, and economic shocks. The final pillar is flexibility. A good legacy system adapts as family needs change. It should allow heirs to refinance, sell, reinvest, or expand without destroying the foundation.

Practical Example: *Creating a Generational Equity System*

Let's look at how this works in real life. Robert owns a home worth $1,000,000 and owes $600,000. Eighty percent of $1,000,000 is $800,000. Subtracting the mortgage leaves $200,000 available for a HELOC. Robert opens the line but only uses $120,000, leaving $80,000 unused as protection.

Robert uses $90,000 to buy two rental properties that together produce $3,000 per month in net cash flow. That equals $36,000 per year. The HELOC interest on $90,000 at 8 percent is $7,200, leaving $28,800 in net income.

Robert uses $20,000 to pay off high-interest family debt. That debt was costing 22 percent, or $4,400 per year. On the HELOC at 8 percent, it costs $1,600. That saves $2,800 per year.

Robert keeps $10,000 in cash.

Now let's add everything up. Robert earns $36,000 from rentals and saves $2,800 from interest reduction, for a total benefit of $38,800. He pays $7,200 plus $1,600 in HELOC interest, totaling $8,800. $38,800 minus $8,800 equals $30,000 in net annual benefit.

Robert uses that $30,000 to pay down the HELOC and mortgage. In four years, the $120,000 HELOC is gone. The rentals remain, producing income for his family. When Robert passes the assets to his heirs, they receive income-producing properties with no debt attached. That is what legacy wealth looks like.

Chapter 10

The Smart Borrower's Lifetime Operating System

This final chapter brings everything together into one integrated system. A smart borrower does not use home equity as a one-time solution to a problem. They use it as a lifetime operating system that adapts as their income, goals, and markets change. This system is what allows ordinary homeowners to behave like professional investors while keeping their family and home protected. When designed correctly, your home equity strategy becomes a financial autopilot that grows, self-corrects, and compounds over decades.

The foundation of the operating system is alignment. Your income, your assets, your debt, and your equity must all be pointed in the same direction. If one part grows while another weakens, the system becomes unstable. Smart borrowers periodically audit their entire financial picture. They look at property values, HELOC limits, interest rates, rental income, business profits, tax strategies, and cash reserves. When something drifts out of balance, it is adjusted before it becomes a problem. This keeps the system smooth and predictable. The second layer is automation. Cash flow should move with minimal friction. Rent, business income, and other profits should be routed into accounts that automatically reduce HELOC balances, fund reserves, and build investment capital. This prevents emotional spending and ensures that progress continues even when life gets busy. A system that relies on willpower eventually breaks. A system that runs on structure lasts.

The third layer is adaptability. Markets change. Interest rates rise and fall. Property values fluctuate. Smart borrowers never assume today's conditions will last. They build optionality into their system by keeping unused credit, maintaining liquidity, and avoiding permanent commitments to variable-rate debt. This allows them to shift strategies when opportunities or risks appear.

The fourth layer is growth sequencing. A lifetime system does not expand all at once. It grows in stages. First, high-interest debt is eliminated. Then income-producing assets are acquired. Then cash flow increases. Then equity regenerates. Then the next expansion begins. Each stage funds the next. This is how homeowners move from stability to wealth without ever putting themselves in danger.

The fifth layer is protection. Insurance, legal structures, reserves, and conservative loan-to-value ratios all exist to protect the system from shocks. Smart borrowers do not build on hope. They build on margins of safety. This allows them to survive recessions, job losses, tenant turnover, and personal emergencies without losing their home or their assets.

The final layer is purpose. The system must serve your life, not the other way around. Whether your goal is freedom, family security, early retirement, or generational wealth, your equity strategy should be aligned with what you want your life to look like. When equity is used with intention, it becomes a tool for designing the life you want rather than reacting to the one you have.

By mastering this operating system, you do not just become someone who understands HELOCs. You become someone who understands how to move money through time. That is the true power of home equity.

Practical Example: *Running a Lifetime Equity Operating System*

Let's see how this looks in practice. Olivia owns a home worth $1,100,000 and owes $650,000 on her mortgage. Eighty percent of $1,100,000 is $880,000. Subtracting the mortgage gives her $230,000 available for a HELOC. Olivia opens the line but only uses $150,000, leaving $80,000 unused as a permanent safety buffer. Olivia uses $90,000 to buy two rental properties that together generate $3,500 per month in net cash flow. That equals $42,000 per year. The HELOC interest on $90,000 at 8 percent is $7,200, leaving $34,800 in net rental income.

Olivia uses $40,000 to invest in a small business that produces $1,200 per month in profit, or $14,400 per year. The interest on $40,000 at 8 percent is $3,200, leaving $11,200 net.

Olivia uses $20,000 to eliminate credit card debt that was charging 20 percent interest. That debt was costing $4,000 per year. On the HELOC at 8 percent, it now costs $1,600, saving $2,400 per year.

Now let's add everything together. Olivia earns $42,000 from rentals and $14,400 from the business, for a total of $56,400. She saves $2,400 from interest reduction, bringing the total benefit to $58,800. She pays $7,200 plus $3,200 plus $1,600 in HELOC interest, totaling $12,000. $58,800 minus $12,000 equals $46,800 in net annual cash flow.

Olivia sends $36,800 of that into the HELOC and keeps $10,000 for lifestyle and reserves. After the first year, her $150,000 HELOC balance drops to $113,200. That creates $36,800 in new available credit without adding risk. Her rentals and business continue producing income, and her system grows stronger every year.

This is the Smart Borrower's Blueprint in action.

Chapter 11

When to Expand, When to Pause, and When to Pull Back

One of the greatest dangers in any leverage-based strategy is not taking action too slowly, but taking it too fast. The smart borrower's greatest advantage is not how much they can borrow, but how well they know when to move and when to wait. This chapter teaches the art of pacing. It explains how to read your own financial signals, market conditions, and cash-flow trends so you can expand your equity system when it is safe, pause when conditions are uncertain, and pull back before problems ever appear.

The first signal is cash-flow coverage. Expansion is only allowed when your existing income comfortably covers your current HELOC payments with margin. Smart borrowers require a safety ratio, meaning their cash flow should exceed debt obligations by at least 30 to 50 percent before they consider taking on more leverage. If income barely covers payments, the system is fragile. When income greatly exceeds payments, the system is ready to grow.

The second signal is liquidity. You should never expand when your cash reserves are low. Liquidity is your shock absorber. If you do not have at least three to six months of HELOC payments and living expenses set aside, you pause. This ensures that one bad month never turns into a crisis.

The third signal is interest-rate trend. When rates are rising quickly, expansion becomes more dangerous. When rates are stable or falling, expansion becomes safer. Smart borrowers do not fight the rate environment. They align with it.

The fourth signal is property value stability. If values are rising or stable, equity grows. If values are falling, equity shrinks. Expansion in a falling market requires more caution and lower loan-to-value usage.

The fifth signal is emotional clarity. Stress, exhaustion, or financial anxiety are signals to slow down. Smart borrowers make their best decisions when calm and focused.

Pulling back is not failure. It is strategy. Paying down balances, increasing reserves, or temporarily halting new investments strengthens the system and prepares it for the next growth phase.

Practical Example: *Using Signals to Control Expansion*

Let's look at a real example. Daniel owns a home worth $900,000 and owes $560,000. Eighty percent of $900,000 is $720,000. Subtracting the mortgage gives $160,000 available for a HELOC. Daniel uses $100,000 and keeps $60,000 unused.

Daniel's investments generate $3,200 per month in net cash flow, which is $38,400 per year. His HELOC interest on $100,000 at 8 percent is $8,000 per year. That leaves $30,400 in net income.

Daniel saves $12,000 per year into cash reserves. He uses $18,400 to pay down the HELOC. After one year, his balance drops to $81,600. His available credit increases.

Now Daniel looks at expansion. His cash flow of $38,400 is almost five times his $8,000 HELOC interest. His reserves are growing. This tells him it is safe to expand.

Daniel uses $20,000 of new available credit to buy another income-producing asset that adds $6,000 per year in profit. The interest on $20,000 at 8 percent is $1,600. He gains $4,400 net. His system grows without stress.

This is how smart borrowers grow on purpose instead of by accident.

Chapter 12

Becoming Financially Unstoppable With a Home Equity Strategy

At this point in the series, you no longer think like a typical homeowner. You think like a capital manager. The purpose of everything you have learned is not to take bigger risks, but to remove financial fragility from your life. When your home equity strategy is structured correctly, you become resilient. You can handle job changes, market shifts, health events, business ups and downs, and even recessions without fear. This chapter is about transforming that resilience into long-term financial dominance — not in the sense of control over others, but in control over your own destiny.

Being financially unstoppable does not mean never losing money or never facing obstacles. It means you always have options. Options come from liquidity, credit, income, and assets working together. A HELOC by itself is not power. A HELOC connected to cash flow, reserves, and appreciating assets is. Smart borrowers never put themselves in a position where one bad event can collapse their system. They build multiple layers of protection and multiple paths forward. The first layer is redundancy. You should never rely on a single income source to service your equity. Rentals, businesses, investments, and employment income should all exist in parallel. If one slows, the others carry the load. This is how you eliminate the risk of financial ruin.

The second layer is speed. When opportunities appear, the person with ready access to capital wins. Because your HELOC is already open and structured, you do not wait for banks, underwriters, or approvals. You move. This allows you to buy discounted assets, rescue distressed deals, and invest when others cannot.

The third layer is patience. Because you are not desperate for money, you can wait for the best opportunities. You do not chase returns. You select them. This is one of the most powerful advantages of a well-run equity system.

The fourth layer is recovery. Even when something goes wrong, your system can heal itself. Cash reserves, unused credit, and multiple income streams allow you to absorb losses without spiraling. You do not need bailouts. You have built your own safety net.

The fifth layer is reinvention. Over time, industries change. Real estate cycles shift. Businesses rise and fall. A smart borrower can exit one strategy and enter another because their capital is flexible. Equity is not locked into one asset forever. It moves. The final layer is legacy. An unstoppable system outlives you. It provides education, income, and opportunity to your family. You are not just building wealth. You are building a financial ecosystem that keeps producing long after you are gone.

Practical Example: *An Unstoppable Equity System in Action*

Let's look at how this works with real numbers. Natalie owns a home worth $1,200,000 and owes $700,000 on her mortgage. Eighty percent of $1,200,000 is $960,000. Subtracting the mortgage gives her $260,000 available for a HELOC. Natalie opens the full line but only uses $160,000, leaving $100,000 unused as a permanent safety reserve.

Natalie uses $100,000 to purchase three rental properties that together generate $4,200 per month in net cash flow. That equals $50,400 per year. The HELOC interest on $100,000 at 8 percent is $8,000, leaving $42,400 in net rental income.

Natalie uses $40,000 to buy a small business that produces $1,800 per month in profit, or $21,600 per year. The interest on $40,000 at 8 percent is $3,200, leaving $18,400 in net business income.

Natalie uses $20,000 to eliminate high-interest debt that was costing 22 percent interest, or $4,400 per year. On the HELOC at 8 percent, that debt now costs $1,600, saving $2,800 per year.

Now let's add everything together. Natalie earns $50,400 from rentals and $21,600 from her business, for a total of $72,000. She also saves $2,800 in interest, bringing her total benefit to $74,800. She pays $8,000 plus $3,200 plus $1,600 in HELOC interest, totaling $12,800. $74,800 minus $12,800 equals $62,000 in net annual cash flow.

Natalie uses $45,000 of that to pay down the HELOC and keeps $17,000 for lifestyle and reserves. After the first year, her $160,000 balance drops to $115,000. Her unused credit grows. Her income continues. Her system becomes stronger every year.

This is what it means to be financially unstoppable with home equity.

Chapter 13

The Smart Borrower's 10-Year Wealth Flight Plan

A true home-equity strategy is not measured in months. It is measured in decades. Most homeowners think about their mortgage in terms of how long it takes to pay off. Smart borrowers think in terms of how many financial lives their equity can create before that mortgage is gone. This chapter introduces the concept of the 10-year wealth flight plan — a clear, structured path that shows how equity, income, appreciation, and reinvestment work together over time to move you from homeowner to capital owner.

The reason so many people fail financially is not lack of income, but lack of direction. They drift from one financial decision to another without knowing where they are going. A flight plan solves this. It defines where you are today, where you want to be in ten years, and what steps must happen each year in between. Your home equity becomes the fuel for that journey.

The first stage of the flight plan is stabilization. This is where high-interest debt is eliminated, cash reserves are built, and a HELOC is opened and structured. During this stage, your goal is not to get rich but to become unbreakable. You want to reach a point where one unexpected event cannot ruin you.

The second stage is income creation. Equity is deployed into assets that generate cash flow. The focus is not on appreciation but on monthly income. Rentals, businesses, and investments funded by equity begin replacing earned income. Every dollar of income that comes from assets instead of labor increases freedom.

The third stage is compounding. Income is used to pay down HELOC balances and fund new investments. Equity regenerates. Assets multiply. Your net worth begins to grow exponentially because both your properties and your income streams are increasing at the same time.

The fourth stage is acceleration. As assets appreciate and loans are paid down, refinancing and HELOC increases allow larger opportunities. You are no longer limited by savings. You are limited only by how fast your system can safely grow.

The final stage is dominance. At this point, your income far exceeds your expenses, your debts are shrinking, and your equity is expanding. Your home is no longer just shelter. It is the command center of a financial empire.

This flight plan turns your house into a launchpad instead of a liability.

Practical Example: *A 10-Year Home Equity Wealth Flight*

Let's see what this looks like with real numbers. Eric owns a home worth $950,000 and owes $550,000. Eighty percent of $950,000 is $760,000. Subtracting the mortgage gives him $210,000 available for a HELOC. Eric opens the line but only uses $140,000, leaving $70,000 unused for protection.

In year one, Eric uses $90,000 to buy two rental properties that produce $3,200 per month in net cash flow, or $38,400 per year. The HELOC interest on $90,000 at 8 percent is $7,200, leaving $31,200 net. Eric uses another $30,000 to eliminate high-interest debt, saving $6,000 per year while paying $2,400 in HELOC interest, netting $3,600.

So in year one, Eric's total financial gain is $31,200 plus $3,600, which equals $34,800. He uses $25,000 of that to pay down the HELOC and keeps the rest as reserves.

After one year, Eric's HELOC balance drops from $120,000 to $95,000. His rentals are still producing income. In year two, rents rise slightly, adding another $2,000 in income. Eric now uses that growing income to pay down another $30,000.

By year five, Eric has paid down most of the original HELOC.

His properties have appreciated, allowing him to increase his HELOC by another $50,000 without increasing risk. He uses that to buy two more rentals.

By year ten, Eric owns multiple income-producing properties, his HELOC is largely paid off, and his home equity has grown through appreciation and debt reduction. His system now generates well over $100,000 per year in passive income.

That is the power of a 10-year home equity flight plan.

Chapter 14

Turning Volatility Into Advantage

Most people fear volatility because they experience it from a position of weakness. Rising rates, falling home prices, inflation, layoffs, and market crashes destroy people who depend on a single income stream or who are fully exposed to debt with no buffer. But for a smart borrower, volatility is not danger — it is opportunity. When your home equity system is properly built, financial turbulence becomes the exact condition that allows you to buy assets cheaper, negotiate better deals, and expand while others retreat. This chapter explains how to position yourself so that chaos in the economy works in your favor instead of against you.

The first principle of volatility advantage is liquidity. When markets are unstable, sellers need speed. Banks tighten lending. Buyers with cash and credit lines dominate. A HELOC that is already open gives you both. You do not wait for approvals while others lose deals. You move while prices are discounted. That is why smart borrowers open HELOCs during calm times, not crises. Volatility is when you deploy, not when you apply.

The second principle is psychological positioning. When markets fall, fear spreads. Most people freeze or sell at the wrong time. Smart borrowers operate from numbers, not emotion. They know their cash flow, reserves, and buffers. They know what they can afford. This allows them to step into opportunities that emotionally paralyzed people cannot touch.

The third principle is asset repricing. In volatile markets, assets temporarily fall below their long-term value. Properties, businesses, and even entire portfolios go on sale. Smart borrowers use equity to buy discounted income streams, not to speculate on short-term price movement. They let time and cash flow do the work.

The fourth principle is interest spread control. Volatility often increases interest rates. Smart borrowers only deploy equity when the income produced by the asset is significantly higher than the interest cost. That spread protects them even if rates rise.

The fifth principle is exit layering. Every asset acquired in volatile times should have multiple exit paths. It must cash flow, appreciate over time, and be sellable if needed. This makes volatility survivable and profitable.

The final principle is patience. Volatility does not happen in one day. It happens in waves. Smart borrowers keep dry powder and wait for the best deals, not the first ones.

Practical Example: *Profiting From Volatility With Home Equity*

Let's see how this works with real numbers. Anthony owns a home worth $1,000,000 and owes $620,000. Eighty percent of $1,000,000 is $800,000. Subtracting the mortgage gives him $180,000 available for a HELOC. Anthony opens the full line but only uses $120,000, leaving $60,000 unused as protection.

A market downturn hits. Property values drop and distressed sellers appear. Anthony uses $90,000 of his HELOC to buy two discounted rental properties. Together they generate $3,800 per month in net cash flow, or $45,600 per year. The HELOC interest on $90,000 at 9 percent in a higher-rate environment is $8,100. That leaves $37,500 in net rental income.

Anthony also uses $20,000 of his HELOC to buy a small business from an owner who needs to sell quickly. The business produces $1,400 per month in profit, or $16,800 per year. The interest on $20,000 at 9 percent is $1,800, leaving $15,000 net.

Anthony uses $10,000 to pay off credit card debt that was costing 24 percent, or $2,400 per year. On the HELOC at 9 percent, it costs $900, saving $1,500.

Now let's add everything. Anthony earns $45,600 from rentals and $16,800 from the business, totaling $62,400. He saves $1,500 from interest reduction, bringing total benefit to $63,900. He pays $8,100 plus $1,800 plus $900 in HELOC interest, totaling $10,800. $63,900 minus $10,800 equals $53,100 in net annual benefit.

Anthony uses $40,000 of that to pay down the HELOC and keeps $13,100 in reserves. After one year, his $120,000 balance drops to $80,000. His properties and business continue producing income, and when markets recover, their values rise. That is how volatility becomes advantage.

Chapter 15

The Smart Borrower's Endgame: Permanent Wealth Without Permanent Debt

The true goal of using home equity is not to become highly leveraged. It is to reach a point where your wealth remains while your debt disappears. This is the endgame of the smart borrower's strategy: a life where income, assets, and financial security exist independently of any loans, yet you still retain access to credit whenever you need it. This chapter shows you how to move from a leveraged growth phase into a debt-light, cash-rich, opportunity-driven phase without dismantling the system you have built.

The endgame begins when cash flow exceeds your living expenses by a comfortable margin. At this point, you no longer depend on your job to survive. That does not mean you stop working; it means you stop being forced. Smart borrowers then shift their focus from acquiring assets to consolidating power. They begin paying down HELOC balances, refinancing properties into long-term fixed-rate loans, and building large reserves. This reduces risk while preserving income. The second step of the endgame is converting growth into stability. Instead of chasing more deals, you optimize what you already own. You raise rents, improve operations, and refinance properties at lower rates or higher values. This frees up equity while lowering monthly obligations. The result is higher cash flow with less risk.

The third step is asset harvesting. Some investments will outperform others. Smart borrowers sell or refinance their top performers and use the proceeds to eliminate remaining debt. This leaves them with fewer assets but far more net worth and far less risk.

The fourth step is capital liberation. Once major debts are gone, your HELOC becomes a true financial safety net. You do not need to use it often, but when opportunities appear, you can deploy it quickly and safely.

The final step is living from returns instead of principal. Your income now comes from rent, businesses, dividends, and interest savings, not from selling assets or borrowing. Your wealth becomes permanent.

Practical Example: *Reaching the Smart Borrower's Endgame*

Let's see how this works with real numbers. Sophia owns a home worth $1,300,000 and owes $700,000. Eighty percent of $1,300,000 is $1,040,000. Subtracting the mortgage gives her $340,000 available for a HELOC. Sophia previously used

$200,000 of that to build a portfolio of rentals and businesses.

Those assets now produce $9,000 per month in net cash flow, which is $108,000 per year. The HELOC interest on $200,000 at 8 percent is $16,000. That leaves $92,000 in net income.

Sophia's living expenses are $60,000 per year. That leaves $32,000 per year to reduce debt. She uses that $32,000 annually to pay down the HELOC. In about six years, the $200,000 balance is gone.

During those six years, her properties appreciate and rents rise. By the time the HELOC is paid off, her assets are worth far more than when she started. Her home equity is fully restored. Her income remains.

Sophia now owns multiple income-producing assets and a home with no HELOC debt. Her income covers her life. Her credit remains available. She has reached the endgame: permanent wealth without permanent debt.

That is the Smart Borrower's Blueprint fulfilled.

Final Thoughts

The journey you have taken through this book is not about learning how to borrow more money. It is about learning how to take control of your financial future using the most powerful asset most people will ever own — their home. Home equity is not just a number on a statement. It is stored opportunity. It is dormant leverage. It is the difference between being trapped by circumstances and being able to act when opportunity appears. By now, you understand that when equity is used without strategy, it creates stress, debt, and regret. When it is used with structure, it creates income, freedom, and long-term wealth.

Most people are taught that debt is dangerous. What they are never taught is that unmanaged debt is dangerous, but strategic debt can be transformative. Throughout this book, you have learned how to separate emotional borrowing from professional capital deployment. You have learned how to build buffers, create income streams, manage risk, and design exit strategies. These are not tricks. They are the same principles used by banks, real estate investors, and financial institutions. The only difference is that you are now using them for your own life instead of for theirs. One of the most important shifts you can make is to stop thinking of your home as something that simply costs you money. A house can either be a liability that drains your income or an asset that funds your future. The difference is not the property — it is the structure around it. When your home is connected to cash flow, reserves, and a disciplined borrowing system, it becomes a financial engine. That engine does not require luck. It runs on planning, numbers, and patience.

The smartest borrowers are not the ones who take the biggest risks. They are the ones who never have to panic. When markets shift, when interest rates rise, or when life throws surprises, they already have credit, cash, and income working for them. They do not scramble for loans. They do not sell assets at the wrong time. They make calm decisions from a position of strength. That is the real goal of everything you have learned here.

As you move forward, remember that the blueprint you now hold is not rigid. It is adaptive. Your income will change. Your goals will evolve. Markets will rise and fall. The beauty of a well-designed equity system is that it moves with you. You can grow. You can slow down. You can pivot. You can retire. You can help your family. You can take opportunities when they appear. Your home equity becomes a lifelong partner instead of a silent bystander. Wealth is not about how much you earn. It is about how long you can remain in control. When your home equity is working for you, you are no longer dependent on a paycheck, a bank's approval, or perfect market conditions. You have built your own financial ecosystem. That is what it means to be a smart borrower.

How to Get a Personalized HELOC Review

If you found *HELOC Fundamentals: How Home Equity Lines of Credit Really Work — and How to Use Them Safely* helpful, you may want to see how these concepts apply to your own home, credit profile, and financial goals.

Every homeowner's situation is unique. Home value, mortgage balance, credit history, income type, and state-specific lending rules all affect how much equity you can access, what type of HELOC you may qualify for, and what terms may be available. The examples in this book are designed to teach how HELOCs work — but your real options can only be determined by reviewing your actual numbers.

If you would like a **no-obligation Home Equity Line of Credit review**, you can request one here:

Website:https://www.nodocsheloc.com

Email:info@FinibiMortgage.com

A licensed mortgage broker will review your information and explain what HELOC and home equity options may be available to you based on your specific situation.

No cost. No pressure. No obligation.

Joseph G. Correa

About the Author

Joseph G. Correa is a licensed mortgage broker and the founder of Finibi Mortgage, a Florida-based brokerage specializing in home equity, real estate investment financing, and alternative lending strategies for homeowners, business owners, and investors. With more than two decades of experience in mortgage lending, underwriting, and financial structuring, Joseph has helped thousands of borrowers access capital using intelligent, low-risk leverage rather than high-interest consumer debt.

Unlike traditional loan officers who focus only on closing transactions, Joseph's approach is rooted in long-term financial strategy. He believes that mortgages, HELOCs, and credit lines should be used as tools for building wealth, protecting cash flow, and creating financial resilience — not as traps that keep families locked into decades of unnecessary interest payments. This philosophy has made him a trusted advisor for entrepreneurs, real estate investors, and self-employed borrowers who need flexible, modern financing solutions that banks often fail to provide.

Joseph is widely known for his expertise in home equity lines of credit, no-documentation and bank-statement loan programs, investor financing, and creative equity-based strategies such as debt-elimination systems and capital recycling. His ability to translate complex lending rules into simple, actionable guidance has helped homeowners turn idle equity into productive capital for investments, businesses, and passive income.

Through his education platform, Finibi Academy, Joseph has trained tens of thousands of students worldwide in credit, mortgage strategy, real estate financing, and financial independence. His courses and books are used by first-time homeowners, seasoned investors, and financial professionals seeking a clearer, more honest understanding of how modern lending really works.

Joseph created *The Home Equity Wealth Series* to give everyday homeowners the same financial knowledge that banks, hedge funds, and institutional investors use to control capital and minimize risk. His mission is simple: to help people stop guessing, stop fearing debt, and start using smart leverage to build real financial freedom.

When he is not structuring loans or writing, Joseph works with families and investors across the United States to design personalized equity strategies that align with their goals, cash flow, and long-term wealth plans.

The Home Equity Wealth Series Roadmap

The Professional Guide to Using Your Home to Build Financial Freedom

The purpose of *The Home Equity Wealth Series* is to give homeowners the same financial tools and strategies used by banks, investors, and institutions—translated into clear, practical guidance for everyday people. Each book builds on the last, taking you from basic understanding to advanced mastery of how to use home equity safely, intelligently, and profitably across every stage of life.

Book 1 — *HELOC Fundamentals*This book gives you the foundation. You will understand how Home Equity Lines of Credit work, how they are structured, how risk is controlled, and how equity becomes usable capital. The books that follow are designed to help you apply that knowledge to your own situation, your income type, your credit profile, and your long-term financial goals.

Book 2 — *How to Qualify for a HELOC* This book shows you how lenders actually evaluate borrowers. You will learn how credit scores, income, property type, and debt ratios affect approval, limits, and interest rates. You will also learn how to position yourself to qualify for the largest possible credit line at the best possible terms.

Book 3 — *HELOCs for Real Estate Investors* This book focuses on using home equity to buy, rehab, refinance, and scale rental properties. It explains how investors use HELOCs for down payments, renovations, and portfolio growth while keeping cash flow positive and risk controlled.

Book 4 — *Self-Employed HELOC Strategies* Designed for business owners, freelancers, 1099 borrowers, and LLCs, this book explains how bank-statement income, business income, and alternative documentation can be used to qualify for home equity even when traditional tax returns do not reflect true cash flow.

Book 5 — *Credit Mastery for HELOC Approval* This book dives deep into credit strategy. You will learn how utilization, credit mix, and reporting behavior affect HELOC limits and pricing—and how to optimize your credit profile specifically for home equity approval.

Book 6 — *No-Doc & Alternative HELOC Programs* This book covers asset-based HELOCs, no-income-verification options, and non-traditional lending programs for high-net-worth, self-employed, or cash-heavy borrowers who do not fit inside standard underwriting models.

Book 7 — *Using a HELOC to Eliminate Debt* This book teaches how to use home equity to replace high-interest credit cards, personal loans, and auto loans with low-interest revolving credit, allowing borrowers to eliminate debt years faster and save tens of thousands of dollars in interest.

Book 8 — *Using a HELOC to Build Wealth* This book shows how homeowners fund investments, businesses, and passive income streams using HELOCs while maintaining liquidity and controlling risk.

Book 9 — *HELOC Risk Management* This book focuses entirely on safety. You will learn how to structure buffers, cash-flow coverage, rate protection, and leverage limits so your home becomes safer over time—not more vulnerable.

Book 10 — *The Smart Borrower's Home Equity Blueprint* The final book ties everything together into a complete lifetime strategy for using home equity as a personal banking system, investment engine, and financial safety net.

Book 11 — *The Cashflow Accelerator Method*

The Cashflow Accelerator Method is the final transformation stage of *The Home Equity Wealth Series*. While the earlier books teach how to access, qualify for, and safely use home equity, this book teaches how to **weaponize cash flow itself** to permanently eliminate debt and create lasting wealth. Together, these books are designed to turn a single asset—your home—into a lifelong financial advantage. Each volume adds another layer of understanding, allowing you to move from homeowner to capital manager, from borrower to strategist, and from financial stress to long-term stability.

This is not about taking more risk.It is about learning how money really works—and using that knowledge to build financial freedom that lasts.

Educational & Financial Disclaimer

This book is provided for **educational and informational purposes only**. The author and publisher are not engaged in rendering legal, tax, accounting, investment, or financial advice. Although the author is a licensed mortgage broker, the information in this book is intended to provide general education about Home Equity Lines of Credit (HELOCs) and home equity strategy, not personalized financial, legal, or lending advice.

Mortgage programs, underwriting guidelines, interest rates, credit requirements, and home equity products vary by lender, investor, state, and economic conditions, and may change at any time without notice. The examples, calculations, and scenarios presented in this book are hypothetical and are for illustration only. They do not represent guaranteed outcomes or actual loan approvals.

Before making any financial decisions, including applying for a HELOC, refinancing, borrowing against home equity, or using credit for investment or debt repayment, readers should consult with a qualified mortgage professional, financial advisor, tax advisor, or attorney who can evaluate their specific situation.

Risk Disclosure

Borrowing against home equity involves risk. A HELOC is secured by your home, which means failure to make required payments could result in foreclosure or loss of property. This book teaches responsible, conservative, and structured use of home equity, but no financial strategy is risk-free.

Readers are solely responsible for their financial decisions. Neither the author nor the publisher makes any warranties, express or implied, about the accuracy, completeness, or applicability of the information in this book to any individual or situation.

www.ingramcontent.com/pod-product-compliance
Ingram Content Group UK Ltd.
Pitfield, Milton Keynes, MK11 3LW, UK
UKHW020157290926
15471UKWH00005B/918

9 798295 576614